GW00361014

Weather Lore

Volume I

Weather in General

Richard Inwards

Weather Lore

A Collection of

Proverbs, Sayings & Rules

Concerning the Weather

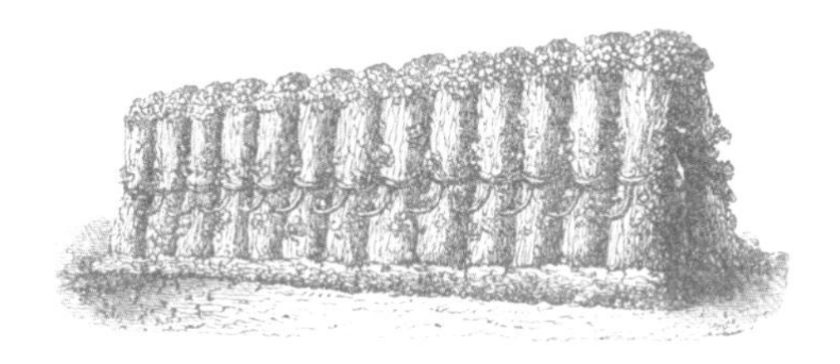

Volume I

Weather in General

Published in Great Britain in 2013 by
Papadakis Publisher

An imprint of New Architecture Group Limited

Kimber Studio, Winterbourne, Berkshire, RG20 8AN, UK
info@papadakis.net | www.papadakis.net

@papadakisbooks PapadakisPublisher

Publishing Director: Alexandra Papadakis
Design: Alexandra Papadakis
Editorial Assistant: Juliana Kassianos

First published in 1898 by Elliot Stock, 62 Paternoster Row, London

ISBN 978 1 906506 35 3

Images for this volume were taken from the publications, with the exception of those that were in the public domain: "Autour De La Lune", "British Birds Vols I & II", "Dictionary of Gardening", "Familiar Wild Flowers", "Le Grandes Inventions Modernes", "La Lecture en Famille", "Le Livre de la Ferme Vols I & II", "Merveilles de la Nature", "Les Merveilles du Monde", "Old Farms, Science For All", "The Fruit Growers Guide Vols I, II & III", "Under the Rainbow Arch", "Universal Instructor Vols I, II & III".

We gratefully acknowledge the permission granted to use these images. Every possible attempt has been made to identify and contact copyright holders. Any errors or omissions are inadvertent and will be corrected in subsequent editions.

A CIP catalogue of this book is available from the British Library

Printed and bound in China

Contents

Introduction

The state of the weather is almost the first subject about which people talk when they meet, and it is not surprising that a matter of such importance to comfort, health, prosperity, and even life itself, should form the usual text and starting-point for the conversation of daily life.

From the earliest times, hunters, shepherds, sailors, and tillers of the earth have from sheer necessity been led to study the teachings of the winds, the waves, the clouds, and a hundred other objects from which the signs of coming changes in the state of the air might be foretold. The weather-wise amongst these primitive people would be naturally the most prosperous, and others would soon acquire the coveted foresight by a closer observance of the same objects from which their successful rivals guessed the proper time to provide against a storm, or reckoned on the prospects of the coming crops. The result has been the framing of a rough set of rules, and the laying down of many "wise saws," about the weather, and the freaks to which it is liable. Some of these observations have settled down into the form of proverbs; others have taken the shape of rhymes; while many are yet floating about, unclaimed and unregistered, but passed from mouth to mouth, as mere records of facts, varying in verbal form according to local idioms, but owning a common origin and purport.

Many weather proverbs contain evidence of keen observation and just reasoning, but a greater number are the offspring of the common tendency to form conclusions from a too limited observation of facts. Even those which have not been confirmed by later experience will be interesting, if only to show the errors into which men may be led by seeing Nature with eyes half closed by prejudice or superstition. It has seemed to me desirable that all this "fossil wisdom" should be collected, and I have endeavoured in this book to present in a systematic form all the current weather lore which is in any way applicable to the climate of the British Isles.

This work is not intended to touch the philosophical aspect of the subject, but it is hoped that its perusal may lead some people to study the weather, not by mere "rule of thumb," as their fathers did, but by intelligent observation, aided by all the niceties of the scientific means now fortunately at the command of everyone.

This collection comprises only those proverbs, sayings, or rules in some way descriptive or prophetic of the weather and its changes, and does not for the most part include those in which the winds, sun, and clouds are only brought in for purposes of comparison and illustration - such, for instance, as, "Always provide against a rainy day," "Every cloud has a silver lining," and others in which the weather is only incidentally or poetically mentioned. Some rhymes have been rejected on account of their being manifestly absurd or superstitious, but the reader will see that much latitude has been allowed in this respect, and, as a rule, all those which may possibly be true will be found in these pages. Predictions as to the peace of the realm, the life and death of kings, etc... founded on the state of the weather for particular days, have of course been left out, as unworthy of remembrance.

A few of the rules here presented will certainly be found to contradict each other, but the reader must judge between them, and assign each its proper value. With regard to those from foreign sources, I have only been able to give a few which seem in some measure applicable to our climate, and it will be seen that even these have lost a great deal of their point in the process of translation.

I have registered the various extracts in the order which seemed most convenient for reference, generally giving precedence to the subjects on which they were the most numerous. Respecting the sources from which they have been derived, I have, of course, availed myself of the collections of general proverbs by Kelly, Howell, Henderson, and Ray. The rest have, for the most part, come under my personal notice, or have been communicated by esteemed correspondents, who are now heartily thanked.

The Bible has handed down to us many proofs of the repute in which weather wisdom was held by the ancients, and it is clear that some of the sacred writers were keen observers of the signs of the sky. The writings of Job are rich in this respect, and contain many allusions to the winds, clouds, and tempests. The New Testament also records some sound weather-lore, and in one instance Christ Himself has not thought it unworthy of Him to confirm a popular adage about a cloud rising in the west and foreshowing rain; for after mentioning the saying, He has added, "And so it is." The Biblical texts referring to the weather have therefore been inserted where appropriate.

In their proper places, too, will be found quotations from learned authors, with Shakespeare at their head. Virgil, Bacon, Thompson, and other less famous men, will be shown to have contributed something to the common stock of information on this subject. Some sound Saxon weather-lore comes also from the mouth of the Shepherd of Banbury, who in the seventeenth century wrote a short list of outdoor signs of coming changes in the state of the air.

It would be strange if all the observations brought in this volume to a common focus did not cast a new ray or two of light on the point to which they have all been directed. Out of so many shots some must hit the mark, though the reader must be warned that even in this "multitude of counsel" there is not absolute safety. These predictions are, after all, but gropings in the dark; and although skilled observers, armed with the delicate instruments contrived by modern science, may be able to forecast with some success the weather for a few hours, yet with respect to the coming months and seasons, or the future harvests and vintages, the learned meteorologist is only on a level with the peasant who watches from the hilltop the "spreadings and driftings of the clouds," or hazards his rude weather guesses from the behaviour of his cattle or the blossoming of the hedge flowers which adorn his paths.

It is perhaps worth mentioning, with respect to those proverbs concerning the weather of particular days, that, on account of the reformation of the calendar, a great many of these sayings must be held to refer to times a little later than the dates now affixed. Notwithstanding this, I have retained the dates which I find by custom attached to the adages, as it is now impossible to say how long before the alteration of the calendar they took their rise. Of course, the real discrepancy will depend on the date of origin, as, in the case of any proverb having been current in the time of Julius Caesar, its date would refer to the same part of the earth's orbit as at present, while the "Saints' Day" proverbs which have been concocted in the Middle Ages would require a correction depending upon the error of the calendar which had accumulated at their date of origin. This alone would account for the uncertain value of all this class of predictions.

The list of times for the flowering of plants must also be taken with some allowances, on account of the varying soil and climate of the different parts of the kingdom from which the information was collected.

Should the reader ask, as he naturally may, to what practical result does all this tend, and how from it he may venture to predict the coming weather, I can only recommend him to try and imbibe the general spirit of the rules and adages, to watch the clouds from a high place, to examine the published weather diagrams, and by collating them try to find where similar results have followed similar indications, and by all the instrumental means he can, go on measuring and gauging heat, pressure, rain, wind, and moisture, in the hope that he may some day arrive at the semblance of a definite law, and the certainty that he is pursuing an interesting and ever-improving study.

I may, however, generally state that those adages which have resulted from the direct observation of clouds, winds and storms are,

as may be supposed, much more to be relied on than all the quips, conceits, and guesses of the would-be weather-wise.

As for this book, it aims at no more than being a manual of outdoor weather wisdom seen from its traditional and popular side, without pretending to any scientific accuracy. Meteorology itself, especially as regards English weather, is very far from having reached the phase of an exact science.

RICHARD INWARDS

Bartholomew Villas,
London, N.W.

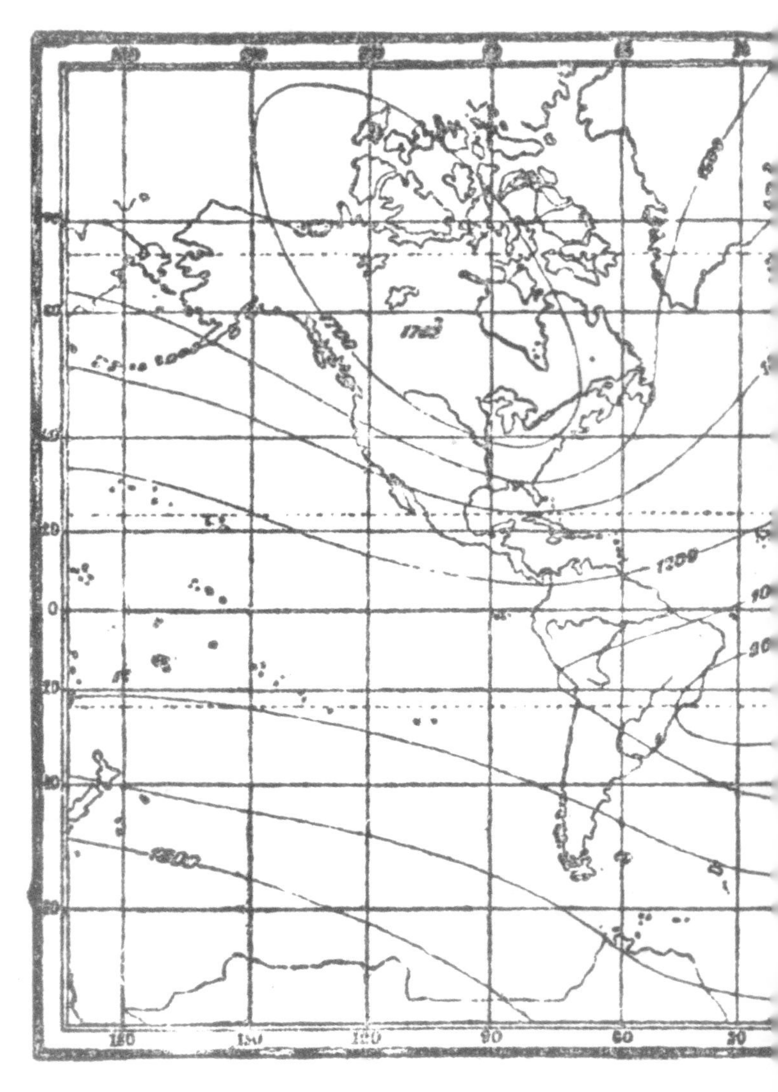
180
150
120
90
60
30
0
20
1200

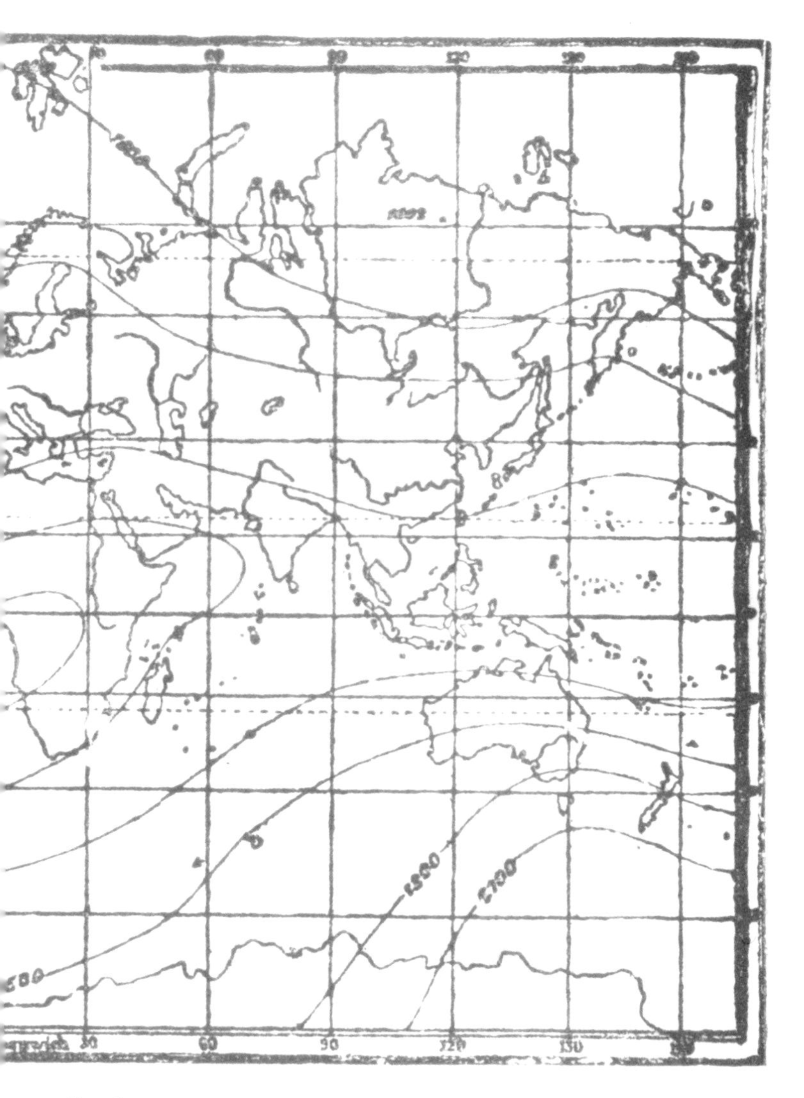

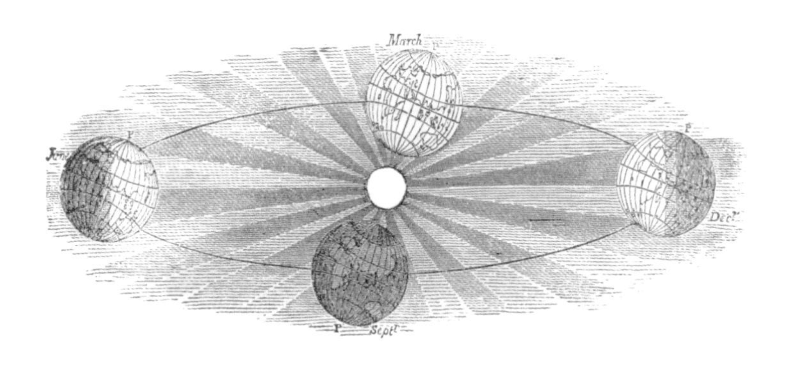
March
Decr
Septr

Weather in General

The weather rules the field. - Spain.

Weather

The almanack-writer makes the almanack,
but God makes the weather. - Denmark.

Almanacks and weather

It is the science of the pure air and the bright heaven, its thoughts are amidst the loveliness of creation, it leads the mind as well as the eye to the morning mist, the noonday glory and the twilight cloud, to the purple peace of the mountain heaven, to the cloudy repose of the green valley; now expatiating on the silence of stormless æther, now on the rushing of the wings of the wind. It is indeed a knowledge which must be felt to be in its very essence full of the soul of the beautiful.
- John Ruskin ("R. Meteorol. Society's Journal", 1839).

Weather study

'Tis not the husbandman, but the good weather,
that makes the corn grow. - T. Fuller.

Good weather

A wise man carries his cloak in fair weather,
and a fool wants his in rain. - Scotland.

Weather caution

When fine take your umbrella;
When raining, please yourself.
- Dr Samuel Johnson.

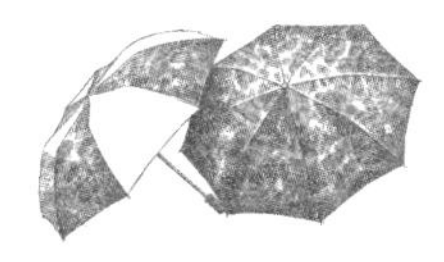

Umbrella

Weather prophecy

Husbandry depended on the periodical rains; and forecasts of the weather, with a view to make adequate provision against a coming deficiency, formed a special duty of the Bráhmans. The philosopher who erred in his predictions observed silence for the rest of his life.
- W. W. Hunter.

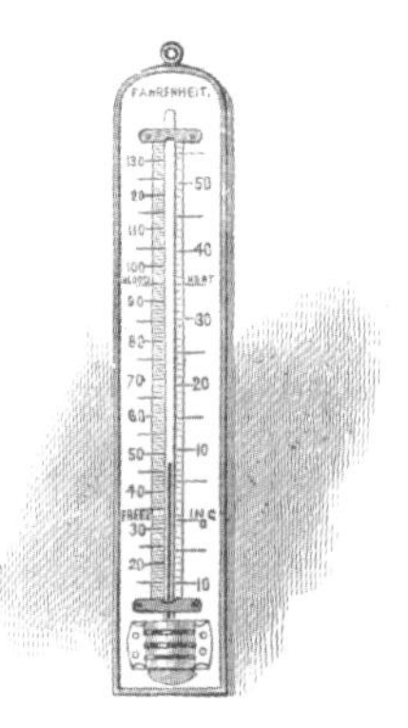

Those who are weather wise
Are rarely otherwise.
- Cornwall.

Weather guesses

To talk of the weather,
it's nothing but folly,
For when it's rain on the hill,
it may be sun in the valley.
- R. Chambers
("Popular Rhymes of Scotland").

Weathers

There are many weathers in five days,
and more in a month.
- Norway.

Proclamation against weather saints

In the reign of Henry VIII, a proclamation was made against the almanacks which transmitted the belief in saints ruling the weather.

Better it is to rise betimes
And make hay while the sun shines,
Than to believe in tales and lies
Which idle people do devise.
Sunshine

Weather, wind, women, and fortune
change like the the moon.
- France

Of Albion's glorious isle, the wonders whilst I write,
The sundry varying soyles, the pleasures infinite;
Where heat kills not the cold, nor cold expells the heat,
Ne calmes too mildly small, nor winds too roughly great;
Nor night doth hinder day, nor day the night doth wrong,
The summer not too short, the winter not too long.
- Drayton.

English climate

Scotland! thy weather's like a modish wife;
Thy winds and rain for ever are at strife;
Like thee, the termagants their blustering try,
And when they can no longer scold, they cry.
- Aaron Hill.

Scottish climate

Whether the weather be fine or wet,
Always water when you set.

Planting weather

Be it dry or be it wet,
The weather'll always pay its debt.

Weather changes

The very air itself and the serenity of heaven will cause some mutation in us according to these verses of Cicero:
The minds of men do in the weather share,
Dark or serene as the day's foul or fair.

Aratus says: "Do not neglect any of these [weather] signs, for it is good to compare a sign with another sign: if two agree, have hope, but be assured still more by a third."
- C. L. Prince.

Weather signs

Times and Seasons

Amongst the first attempts at weather guesses, those concerning the seasons and their probable fitness for agriculture, the breeding of animals, or the navigation of the seas would take a prominent place. The weather during the winter and spring seems to have been narrowly watched, and the chances of a good harvest, a fat pasture, or a loaded orchard inferred from the experience of previous years, combined with a fair reliance upon fortune. Some of these predictions, though not strengthened by modern observation, are not to be altogether despised or thrown aside. They at least show us what kind of weather our forefathers wished to take place and thought most useful at the times to which they refer. The sayings of French, Scotch, and English agree in many particulars - such, for instance, as those referring to Candlemas Day and the early part of February generally. Some of these old sayings are also interesting as perhaps indicating the slowly changing climate of this country, and it is not unlikely that at some distant date most of the predictions will be found inapplicable. Particular saints' days have also been selected as exerting special influence over the weather, and here we are constantly treading on the fringes of the veil of superstition, spread by ignorance over all matters about which but little certain knowledge existed. There are, however, still believers in St. Swithin and St. Valentine as weather prophets; and if their favourites do sometimes fail to bring the expected changes, they have at least no worse guides than those furnished by the Old Moores and Zadkiels of modern times.

It has been thought advisable to admit the proverbs concerning the proper seasons for sowing, etc.; and a table of the times of the flowering of certain well-known plants has been added, so that the progress of the seasons may be watched by observing the punctuality of the vegetable world in heralding their approach.

Note on New Style. - In considering the weather proverbs regarding certain days, it must be remembered that the new style came into use on the day following September 2nd, 1752, which next day was called September 14th, and the eleven dates which would have been called September 3rd, 4th, 5th, 6th, 7th, 8th, 9th, 10th, 11th, 12th and 13th, were omitted from the calendar by Act 24 George II. c. 23.

YEAR

Do not abuse the year till it has passed. - Spain.

Harvest

The harvest depends more on the year than on the field. - Denmark.

Dry

A dry year never beggars the master. - France.

A dry year never starves itself.

If there be neither snow nor rain,
Then will be dear all kinds of grain.

A bad year comes in swimming. - France.

If the old year goes out like a lion, …

Old year

… the new year will come in like a lamb.

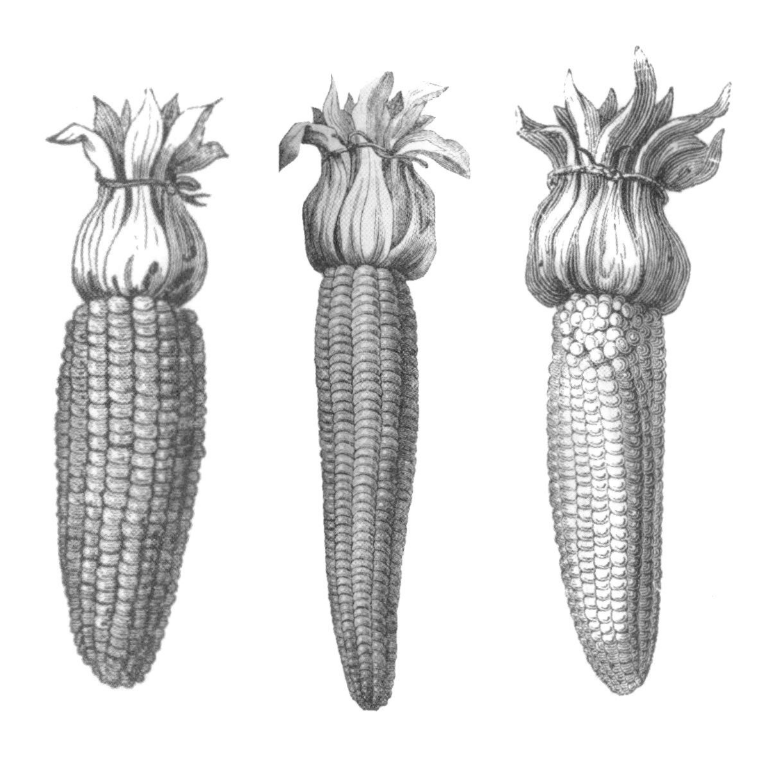

Wet

After a wet year a cold one.

Rainy year, fruit dear.
- Haute Loire.

Wet and dry

Wet and dry years come in triads.

Fine

There are more fine days than cloudy ones in the year.
- Ovid.

Misty

Misty year, year of cornstalks.
- Spain.

Frosty

Year of frosts, year of cornstacks.
- Spain.

Frost year,
Fruit year.
- Eure et Loire.

Frost year,
Wheat year.
- France.

Snowy

Year of snow,
Fruit will grow.
- Milan.

A year of snow, a year of plenty.
- Spain and France.

Windy

A year of wind is good for fruit. - Calvados.

Acorns and figs	Acorn year, purse year. Fig year, worse year. - Spain.
Nuts	A good nut year, a good corn year. Year of nuts, Year of famine. - France (Haute Marne).
Hay	A good hay year, a bad fog year.
Grass	A year of grass good for nothing else. - Switzerland.
Pears Cherries and plums	A pear year, A dear year. A cherry year, A merry year. A plum year, A dumb year. - Kent.
Plums	In the year when plums flourish all else fails. - Devonshire.
Gooseberries	Year of gooseberries, year of bottles [good vintage]. - France.
Haws	A haw year, A braw year. - Ireland and Scotland.

A haw year,
A snaw year. - Scotland.

Mushrooms

Year of mushrooms,
Year of poverty.
- France
(Hautes Pyrénées).

Radishes

Year of radishes,
Year of health.
- Ardèche.

Cows

A cow year a sad year;
A bull year, a glad year.
- Holland.

Corn and cattle

Corn and horn go together.

Leap

Leap year was ne'er a good sheep year.
- Scotland.

SEASONS

A serene autumn denotes a windy winter; a windy winter, a rainy spring; a rainy spring, a serene summer; a serene summer, a windy autumn, so that the air on a balance is seldom debtor to itself. - Lord Bacon.

Satire on seasons

Spring. Slippy, drippy, nippy.
Summer. Showery, flowery, bowery.
Autumn. Hoppy, croppy, poppy.
Winter. Wheezy, sneezy, breezy.
- Attributed to Sydney Smith.
[Composed as a satirical mistranslation of the names given to the months at the time of the French Revolution. - G. F. Chambers.]

Extreme

Extreme seasons are said to occur from the sixth to the tenth year of each decade, especially in alternate decades.

The first three days of any season rule the weather of that season.

The general character of the weather during the last twenty days of March, June, September, or December will rule the following seasons.

SPRING

Spring is both father and mother to us. - Galicia.

Late

A late spring is a great blessing.

A late spring never deceives.

Better late spring and bear, than early blossom and blast.

When the cuckoo comes to the bare thorn,
Sell your cow and buy your corn;
But when she comes to the full bit,
Sell your corn and buy your sheep;
i.e. A late spring is bad for cattle, and an early spring is bad for corn.

If the spring is cold and wet,
then the autumn will be hot and dry.

Cold

A dry spring, rainy summer. - France.

Dry

A wet spring, a dry harvest.

Damp	Spring rain damps, autumn rain soaks. - Russia. In spring a tub of rain makes a spoonful of mud. In autumn a spoonful of rain makes a tub of mud.
Thunder	Thunder in spring Cold will bring.
First thunder	First thunder in spring, if in the south, it indicates a wet season; if the north, a dry season.
Early thunder	Early thunder, early spring.
Lightning	Lightning in spring indicates a good fruit year.
Storms	As the days grow longer, The storms grow stronger.
Spring	As the day lengthens, The cold strengthens. - Yorkshire.

If there's spring in winter, and winter in spring,
The year won't be good for anything.

Spring in winter

There are a hundred days of easterly wind in the first half of the year. - West of England.

Spring and summer

If the spring and summer are dry, the early autumn, and the late autumn as well, are close and free from wind. - Greece
(Theophrastus: "Signs, etc." J. G. Wood's Translation).

SUMMER

Generally a moist and cool summer portends a hard winter. - Bacon.

Moist

An English summer, two hot days and a thunderstorm.

Stormy

A dry summer never made a dear peck.

Dry

A dry summer never begs its bread. - Somerset.

Whoso hath but a mouth
Will ne'er in England suffer drought.

Drought never bred dearth in England.

A mild, wet winter always follows
an unproductive summer.
- Professor Boerne's Latin MS. 1677-1799.

Unproductive

Swallows One swallow does not make a summer.

Rain

Midsummer rain
Spoils hay and grain.

Midsummer rain
Spoils wine stock and grain.
- Portugal.

A wet summer almost always precedes a cold, stormy winter, because evaporation absorbs the heat of the earth. As a wet summer is favourable to the growth of the blackthorn, whenever this shrub is laden with fruit a cold winter may be predicted.
- Professor Boerne's Latin MS. 1677-1799.

Rainy There can never be too much rain before midsummer.
- Sweden.

Happy are the fields that receive summer rain.

In summer a fog from the south, warm weather; from the north, rain.

Fog

A cool summer and a light weight in the bushel.

Cool

If we do not get our Indian summer in October or November, we shall get it in the winter. - United States.

Indian

Summer comes with a bound; winter comes yawning. - Finland.

Summer and winter

As the days begin to shorten,
The heat begins to scorch them.

Days

AUTUMN

A fair and dry autumn brings in always a windy winter. - Pliny.

Dry

Dry vintage, good wine. - Spain.

Clear autumn, windy winter;
Warm autumn, long winter.

Autumn and winter

If the early autumn is mild, the sheep generally suffer from famine.
- Greece (Theophrastus: "Signs, etc." J. G. Wood's Translation).

Early

Late	If the late autumn is unusually bright, the spring is cold as a general rule. - Greece (Theophrastus: "Signs, etc." J. G. Wood's Translation).
Wet	A wet autumn followed by a mild winter is the forerunner of a dry, cold spring. - Professor Boerne's Latin MS., 1677-1799.
	A wet fall indicates a cold and early winter.
Moist	A moist autumn with a mild winter is followed by a cold and dry spring, retarding vegetation.
Fog	Much fog in autumn, much snow in winter.
Thunder	Thunder in the fall indicates a mild, open winter.
Long harvest	A long harvest, a little corn.
Fruit	If you would fruit have, You must bring the leaf to the grave [i.e. transplant in autumn].
Nights	The autumn night is changeable. - Norway.
Winds	If, during the autumn, the winds have been mainly from the south-east, or if the temperature has been lower than usual, it generally rains a great deal about the end of the year. - Professor Boerne's Latin MS. 1677-1799.

WINTER

Winter never rots in the sky. - Italy.

Winter never died in a ditch.

Dry

Winter finds out what summer lays up.

A green winter makes a fat churchyard.

Green

When there is a spring in the winter, or a winter in the spring, the year is never good.

Summer in winter, and summer's flood,
Never boded an Englishman good.

Mild

An abundant wheat crop does not follow a mild winter. - Farmer (Quoted in Notes and Queries, February 27th, 1869).

A warm and open winter portends a hot and dry summer. - Bacon.

One fair day in winter makes not birds merry.

Winter fair day

A fair day in winter is the mother of a storm. - C. Harvey.

An unusually fine day in winter is known locally as a "borrowed day", to be repaid with interest later in the season, known also as a "weather-breeder", and by sailors as a "fox" - Roper.

Fine day in

Fine

Nobody complains about a hundred fine days in winter. - China.

Mild

A warm winter and cool summer never brought a good harvest. - France.

Whae doffs his coat on winter's day
Will gladly put it on in May.
- Scotland.

A mild winter makes a full graveyard. - China.

If the ice will bear a goose before Christmas, it will not bear a duck after.

If the winter sets in early it closes early, but the spring will be fair; but if the contrary the spring also will be late. If the winter is wet, the spring is dry; if the winter is dry, the spring is fair.
- Greece (Theophrastus: "Signs, etc." J. G. Wood's Translation).

Clear

Neither give credit to a clear winter nor a cloudy spring.

Long

Long winter and late spring are both good for hay and grain, but bad for corn and garden.

Rainy

After a rainy winter follows a fruitful spring.

Floods

Winter will not come till the swamps are full.
- Southern United States.

Wet

If there is much rain in the winter, the spring is generally dry. If the winter is dry, the spring is rainy. - Greece
(Theophrastus: "Signs, etc." J. G. Wood's Translation).

Thunder

Winter thunder and summer flood
Never boded an Englishman good.

Winter thunder,
Rich man's good and poor man's hunger
[i.e. it is good for fruit and bad for corn].

Winter storm

If in winter the barometer rises very high, and a thick fog sets in, it is a sure sign that the south-west and north-east winds are "fighting each other." Neither of them can make head against the other, and there is a calm, but there is great danger of such a state of things being followed by a bad gale.
- United States.

When the winter solstice has not been preceded nor followed by the usual storms, the following summer will be dry at least five times out of six.
- Professor Boerne's Latin MS. 1677-1799.

Fog

A winter fog
Will freeze a dog.

Frost

Mony a frost and mony a thowe [thaw]
Soon maks mony a rotten yowe [ewe].

Darkness

If at the beginning of winter there is dark weather and heat, and these pass away under the influence of winds without rain, it indicates that hail will follow towards spring.
- Theophrastus ("Signs, etc." J. G. Wood's Translation).

Midwinter

A seven-night before midwinter day and as much after, the sea is allayed and calm. - Pliny.

JANUARY

The blackest month in all the year
Is the month of Janiveer.

A favourable January brings us a good year.
The month of January is like a gentleman (as he begins, so he goes on). - Spain.

In Janiveer if the sun appear, — Bright
March and April pay full dear.
January warm, the Lord have mercy! — Warm

A summerish January, a winterish spring.

If you see grass in January, — Grass
Lock your grain in your granary.

If the grass grow in Janiveer,
It grows the worse for it all the year.

January flowers do not swell the granary. — Flowers
- Spain.

January blossoms fill no man's cellar. — Blossoms
- Portugal.

If birds begin to whistle in January, frosts to come. — Birds
- Rutland.

When gnats swarm in January, the peasant becomes a beggar. — Gnats
- Holland.

Mild

If January calends be summerly gay,
It will be winterly weather till the calends of May.

Spring

A January spring is worth naething. - Scotland.

Dry

Dry January, plenty of wine.
A wet January, a wet spring.

Wet

A wet January is not so good for corn,
but not so bad for cattle.
- Spain and Portugal.

January wet, no wine you get.

In January much rain and little snow is bad for mountains, valleys, and trees.

Much rain in January,
no blessing to the fruit.

Thaw

Always expect a thaw in January.

Fog

Fog in January brings a wet spring.

Snow

If there is no snow before January,
there will be the more in March and April.

As the day lengthens,
So the cold strengthens.

A kindly, good Janiveer
Freezeth the pot by the fire. - Tusser.

Jack Frost in Janiveer
Nips the nose of the nascent year.

Frost

Hoar-frost and no snow is hurtful to fields, trees, and grain.

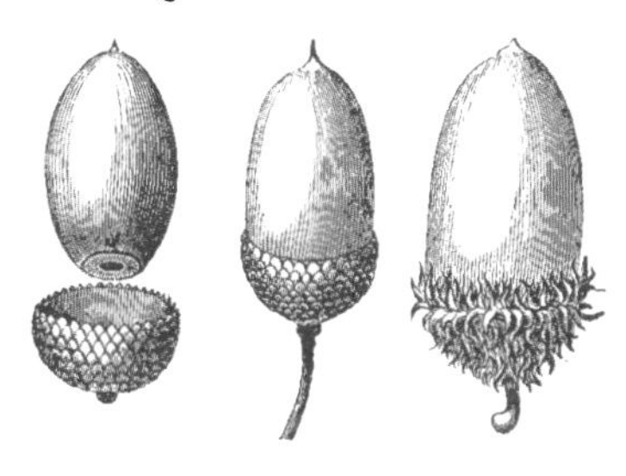

When oak-trees bend with snow in January, good crops may be expected.

Oaks

A January chicken is sold dearly or dies. - Spain.

Chickens

Thunder in January signifieth the same year great winds, plentiful of corn and cattle, peradventure. - "Book of Knowledge."

Thunder

January and following months

A cold January, a feverish February, a dusty March, a weeping April, and a windy May, presage a good year and gay. - France.

January and May sowing

Who in January sows oats
Gets gold and groats;
Who sows in May
Gets little that way.

January and May

January commits the fault and May bears the blame. [Applied in metaphor to human affairs also.]

A warm January, a cold May.

Jan 1st

Morning red, foul weather and great need.

1st, 2nd, 3rd

The first three days of January rule the coming three months.

3rd

It will be the same weather for nine weeks as it is on the ninth day after Christmas. - Sweden.

6th

At twelfth day, the days are lengthened a cock's stride. - Italy.

12th

If on January 12th the sun shine, it foreshows much wind. - Shepherd's Almanack, 1676.

14th

January 14th, St. Hilary,
The coldest day of the year. - Yorkshire.

January 14th will either be the coldest or wettest
day of the year.
- Huntingdonshire.

Remember on St. Vincent's Day,
If that the sun his beams display,
Be sure to mark his transient beam,
Which through the casement sheds a gleam;
For 'tis a token bright and clear
Of prosperous weather all the year.

St. Vincent opens the seed.
- Spain.

At St. Vincent all water is good as seed.
- Spain.

If the sun shine on January 22nd,
there shall be much wind.
- Husbandman's Practice.

On St. Vincent's Day the vine sap rises to
the branch, but retires frightened if it find frost.
- France.

If St. Vincent's has sunshine,
One hopes much rye and wine;
If St. Paul's is bright and clear, 25th
One does hope a good year.

Fair on St. Paul's conversion day
is favourable to all fruits.

If St. Paul's Day be fine,
the year will be the same.
- France.

If the sun shine on St. Paul's Day, it betokens a good year; if rain or snow, indifferent; if misty, it predicts great dearth; if thunder, great winds and death of people that year.
- Shepherd's Almanack, 1676.

19th to 31st — The last twelve days of January rule the weather for the whole year.

FEBRUARY

Cold — Februeer
Doth cut and shear.

Mad — Mad February takes his father
into the sunshine and beats him.
- Spain.

Fine — There is always one fine week in February.

All the months in the year
Curse a fair Februeer.

When gnats dance in February,
the husbandman becomes a beggar.

One would rather see a wolf in February than a
peasant in his shirt-sleeves.
- Germany

It is better to see a troop of wolves
than a fine February.
- France.

Isolated fine days in February are known in Surrey
as "weather-breeders", and are considered as certain
to be followed by a storm.

If bees get out in February,
the next day will be
windy and rainy.
- Surrey.

A February spring is not worth a pin.
- Cornwall.

If in February the midges dance on the dunghill,
then lock up your food in the chest.

Rain

If in February there be no rain,
'Tis neither good for hay nor grain.
- Spain and Portugal.

February rain is only good to fill ditches.
- France.

February rain is as good as manure.
- France.

When it rains in February, it will be
temperate all the year. - Spain.

When it rains in February, all the year suffers.

Snow

If February give much snow,
A fine summer it doth foreshow.
- France

Snow which falls in the month of February
puts the usurer in a good humour.
- Italy.

Snow in February
Puts little wheat in the granary.
- France.

In February if thou hearest thunder,
Thou wilt see a summer's wonder.

Thunder

Thunder in February or March,
poor sugar [maple] year.

Whenever the latter part of February
and beginning of March are dry,
there will be a deficiency of rain up to
Midsummer Day.
- C. L. Prince.

When the cat in February
lies in the sun, she will creep
behind the stove in March.
When the north wind does
not blow in February, it will
surely come in March.

February and May	Fogs in February mean frosts in May.
	For every thunder with rain in February there will be a cold spell in May.
February and June	There will be as many frosts in June As there are fogs in February.
February winds	Violent north winds in February herald a fertile year.
February 1st	As long as the sunbeam comes in on Bridget's feast-day, the snow comes before May Day. - Isle of Man.
Feb 2nd (Candlemas)	On the eve of Candlemas Day Winter gets stronger or passes away. - France.
	Snow at Candlemas Stops to handle us. - Rutland.

On Candlemas Day
You must have half your straw
and half your hay.

On Candlemas Day
The good goose begins to lay.

At Candlemas Day
Another winter is on his way. - France.

If Candlemas Day be fine and clear,
Corn and fruits will then be dear.

If Marie's purifying daie,
Be cleare and bright with sunnie raie,
Then frost and cold shall be much more
After the feast than was before.
- A. Fleming.

If it neither rains nor snows on Candlemas Day,
You may straddle your horse and go and buy hay.
- Lincolnshire.

On Candlemas Day the bear, badger, or
woodchuck comes out to see his shadow at noon:
if he does not see it, he remains out; but if he does
see it, he goes back to his hole for six weeks, and
cold weather continues for six weeks longer.
- United States.

If the ground-hog is sunning himself on the 2nd, he
will return for four weeks to his winter quarters again.

The badger peeps out of his hole on Candlemas
Day, and when he finds snow walks abroad, but
if he sees the sun shining he draws back into his hole.
- Germany.

At the day of Candlemas,
Cold in air and snow on grass;
If the sun then entice the bear from his den,
He turns round thrice and gets back again.
- France.

The shepherd would rather see the wolf enter
his fold on Candlemas Day than the sun.
- Germany.

As far as the sun shines in at the window on Candlemas Day, so deep will the snow be ere winter is gone.

If Candlemas Day be fair and bright,
Winter will have another flight.
But if Candlemas Day bring clouds and rain,
Winter is gone and won't come again.
If Candlemas Day be mild and gay,
Go saddle your horses, and buy them hay;
But if Candlemas Day be stormy and black
It carries the winter away on its back.

Good weather on this day indicates a long continuance of winter, and a bad crop; on the contrary, if foul it is a good omen. - Isle of Man.

February 2nd, bright and clear,
Gives a good flax year.

As long before Candlemas as the lark is heard to sing, so long will he be silent afterwards on account of the cold. - Germany.

If a storm on February 2nd, spring is near; but if that day be bright and clear, the spring will be late.

If it snows on February 2nd, only so much as may be seen on a black ox, then summer will come soon.

On Candlemas Day, if the thorns hang a-drop,
Then you are sure of a good pea crop. - Sussex.
[There is a similar proverb with respect to beans.]

If on February 2nd the goose find it wet, then the sheep will have grass on March 25th.

When drops hang on the fence on February 2nd, icicles will hang there on March 25th.

When the wind's in the east on Candlemas Day,
There it will stick till the 2nd of May.

When it rains at Candlemas,
the cold is over. - Spain.

When Candlemas Day is come and gone,
The snow lies on a hot stone.

12th (St. Eulalie)	If the sun smile on St. Eulalie's Day, It is good for apples and cider, they say. - France.
14th (St. Valentine)	To St. Valentine the spring is a neighbour. - France.
	Winter's back breaks about the middle of February.
20th to 28th	The nights of this part of February are called in Sweden "steel nights", on account of their cutting severity.

The night of St. Peter shows what weather we shall have for the next forty days. — 22nd

24th (St. Matthias)

St. Matthias,
Sow both leaf and grass.

If it freezes on St. Matthias' Day,
it will freeze for a month together.

St. Matthias breaks the ice;
if he finds none, he will make it.

St. Matthie
Sends sap into the tree.

The fair of Auld Deer [third Thursday in February] is the warst day in a' the year.
- Aberdeen.

MARCH

March yeans the lammie
And buds the thorn,
And blows through the flint
Of an ox's horn. - Northumberland.

In beginning or in end
March its gifts will send.

March was so angry with an old woman (according to a saying in the island of Kythnos) for thinking he was a summer month, that he borrowed a day from his brother February, and froze her and her flocks to death.
- T. Bent (Greece).

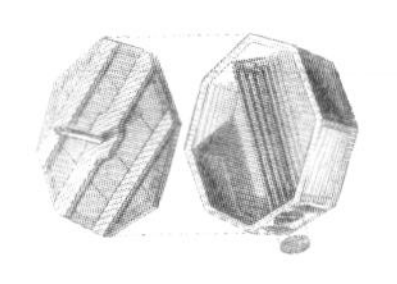

Good riddance, old March!
Now my flock will be full of milk.
An old woman was said to have been frozen to death in April for her impiety in saying this.
- Greece (Wm. J. Woodhouse's "Aetolia").

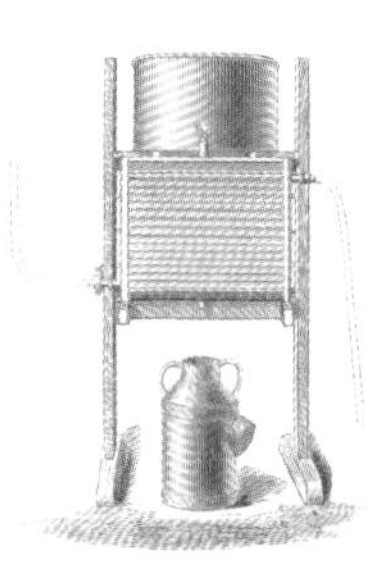

A peck of March dust and a shower in May
Make the corn green and the fields gay.

March dust and March win'
Bleach as well as simmer's sin. - Scotland.

March dust on an apple leaf
Brings all kinds of fruit to grief.
- Herefordshire.

Dry

A load of March dust is worth a ducat.
- Germany.

A bushel of March dust is a thing
Worth the ransom of a king.

A March without water
Dowers the hind's daughter.
- France.

Dry and wet

March dry, good rye;
March wet, good wheat.
- Suffolk.

Mild

March flowers
Make no summer bowers.

Better slaughter in the country than
March should come in mild.
- Isle of Man.

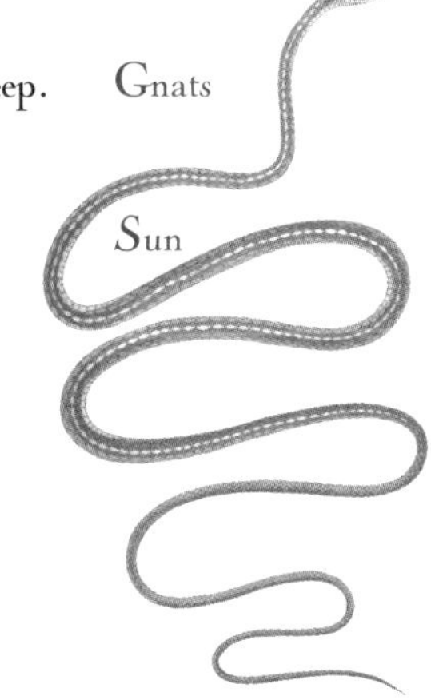

Gnats

When gnats dance in March, it brings death to sheep.
- Holland.

Sun

The March sun raises, but dissolves not.
- G. Herbert.

March sun strikes like a hammer. - Spain.

Better to be bitten by a snake
Than to feel the sun in March.
- Wiltshire.

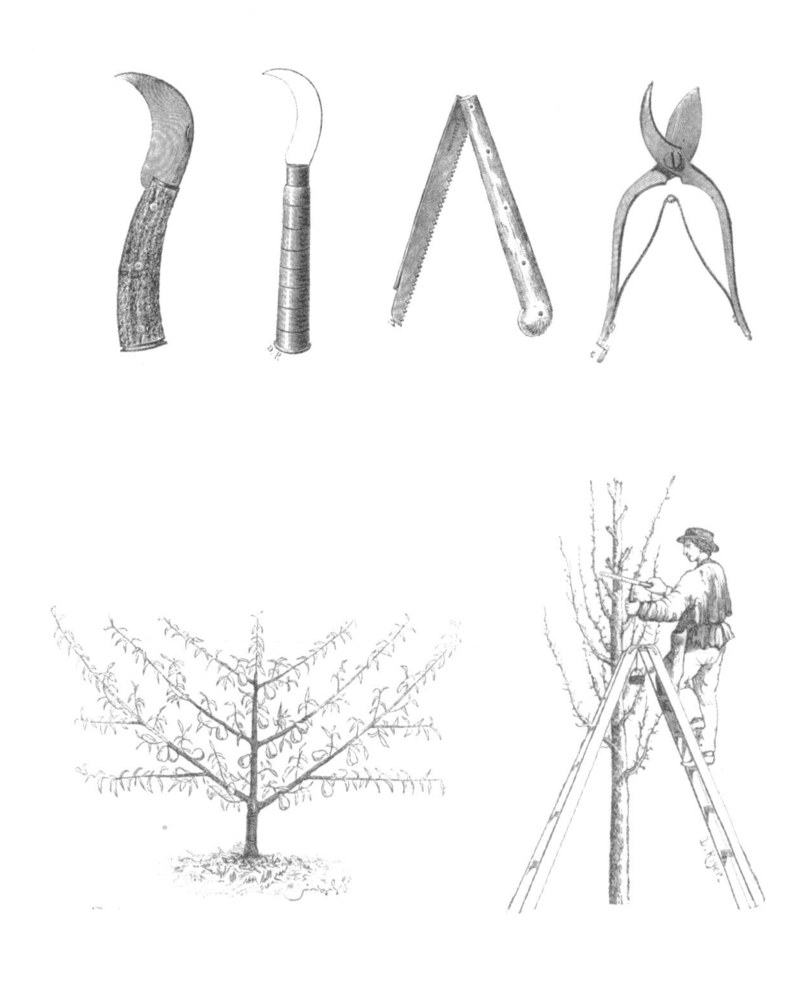

Pruning

**He who freely lops in March
will get his lap full of fruit.
- Portugal.**

Fishing

A March wisher [or whisher]
Is never a good fisher.
- Scotland. [Meaning, a windy
March betokens a bad fish year.]

Wet and warm

March damp and warm
Will do farmer much harm.

Snow

Snow in March is bad for fruit and grape vine.

In March much snow,
To plants and trees much woe. - Germany.

Thunder

Thunder in March betokens a fruitful year. - Germany

When it thunders in March, we may cry "Alas!" - France.

Stormy

March, black ram,*
Comes in like a lion and goes out like a lamb.

March comes in like a lamb and goes out like a lion.
[Reverse of the usual proverb.]

March comes in with adders' heads and goes out with peacocks' tails. - Scotland.

* An obscure expression [Aries?], sometimes "balkham", "backham", or "hackham".

As Mars hasteneth all the humours feel it.

Humours

When March has April weather,
April will have March weather.
- France.

March and April

What March will not
April brings alway.
What April cannot do
May will do all day.
- South Germany.

A dry March, a wet April, a dry May and a wet June, Is commonly said to bring all things in tune.
- Ellis's Modern Husbandman.

March, April, May and June

A windy March
and a rainy April
make a beautiful May.

March, April and May

So many mists in March you see,
So many frosts in May will be.

Mists

March rainy, April windy, and then June
will come beautiful with flowers.
- Spanish.

March, April and June

March search, April try;
May will prove if you live or die.

March, April and May

March winds and April showers
Bring forth May flowers.

A dry March, wet April, and cool May
Fill barn, cellar, and bring much hay.

As it rains in March, so it rains in June.

March and June

Fog in March, thunder in July.

March and July

As much fog in March, so much rain in summer.

A wet March makes a sad August.

March and August

As much dew in March, so much fog rises in August.

Moon

A Saturday's moon in March is enough for
seven years. - Isle of Man.

March 1st (St David's Day)

Upon St. David's Day
Put oats and barley in the clay.

1st and 2nd (St. David, St. Chad)

David and Chad,
Sow peas good or bad;
If they're not in by Benedick [March 21],
They had better stop in the ricke.
- The Country Month by Month.

First comes David, then comes Chad,
And then comes Winneral as though he was mad.
White or black or old house thack.
[Note. Meaning snow, rain, or wind,
the latter endangering the thack or thatch.]

10th

If it does not freeze on the 10th,
a fertile year may be expected.

Mists or hoar-frosts on this day betoken a plentiful
year, but not without some diseases.

15th

On March 15th come sun and swallow.
- Spain.

17th
(St. Patrick)

St. Patrick's Day, the warm side of a stone turns
up, and the broad-back goose begins to lay.

19th
(St. Joseph)

Is't on St. Joseph's Day clear,
So follows a fertile year.

25th
(Lady Day)

Is't on St. Mary's bright and clear,
Fertile is said to be the year.

March borrows of April
Three days, and they are ill;
April borrows of March again
Three days of wind and rain.
The warst blast comes in the
borrowing days.

APRIL

Blackthorn winter

There are generally some warm days at the end of March or beginning of April, which bring the blackthorn into bloom, and which are followed by a cold period called the blackthorn winter.

Beware the blackthorn winter.

A dry April
Not the farmer's will.
April wet
Is what he would get.

Rain

In April each drop counts for a thousand.
- Spain.

April showers
bring summer flowers.

An April flood carries away
the frog and his brood.

Flood

A cold April
The barn will fill.

Cold

A cold April, much bread
and little wine. - Spain.

April cold and wet fills barn and barrel.

A cold and moist April fills the cellar and fattens the cow.
- Portugal.

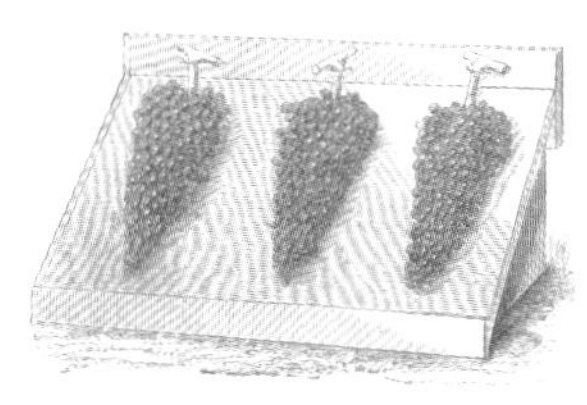

A sharp April kills the pig.

April snow breeds grass.

Till April's dead
Change not a thread.

Frosty	It is not April without a frosty crown. - French.
Change	April weather, Rain and sunshine, both together.
Buds	Vine that buds in April Will not the barrel fill. - France.
Fog	Fogs in April foretell a failure of the wheat-crop next year. - Alabama.
Oak	You must look for grass in April on the top of an oak. Because the grass seldom springs well before the oak begins to put forth. - Ray.
Potatoes	Plant your 'taturs when you will, They won't come up before April. - Wiltshire.
April and March	Whatever March does not want April brings along.

April and
March snows
April and
May

Snow in April is manure; snow in March devours.

A swarm of bees in April for me, and one in May for my brother. - Spain.

Betwixt April and May if there be rain,
'Tis worth more than oxen and wain.

April and May between them make bread for all the year. - Spain.

Cloudy April, dewy May. - France.

April rains for men, May for beasts.
[i.e. a rainy April is good for corn,
and a wet May for grass crops.]

Let it rain in April and May for me,
And all the rest of the year for thee.
- Spain.

April showers bring forth May flowers.

April and June

Moist April, clear June.

April and autumn

The dews of April and May
Make August and September gay.
- France.

After warm April and October,
a warm year next.

Thunder

Thunderstorm in April
is the end of hoar-frost.

When April blows his horn,
It's good for hay and corn.

If it thunders on All Fools' Day
It brings good crops of corn and hay.

First three days

If the first three days in April be foggy,
Rain in June will make the lanes boggy.

3rd

The 3rd of April comes with the cuckoo and the nightingale.

Cuckoo

In April, cuckoo sings her lay;
In May, she sings both night and day;
In June, she loses her sweet strain;
In July, she flies off again.
- North Yorkshire.

15th

This day is called Swallow Day, because swallows ought to appear at this date.

23rd (St. George)

If on St. George's Day the birch leaf is the size of a farthing, on the feast of our Lady of Kazan you will have corn in the barn.
- Russia.

When on St. George rye will hide a crow,
a good harvest may be expected.

At St. George the meadow turns to hay.

St. George cries "Goe!"
St. Mark cries "Hoe!"

25th (St. Mark) — As long before St. Mark's Day as the frogs are heard croaking, so long will they keep quiet afterwards.

MAY

Trust not a day Ere birth of May. - Luther.

For a warm May
The parsons pray.
[Meaning more burial-fees
- a libellous proverb.]

Flowers — Blossoms in May
Are not good, some say.

Damp — May damp and cool fills the barns and wine-vats.

Wet

The haddocks are good
When dipped in May flood.

Three dips in May flood
Mak a' the fish in the sea good.
- Scotland.

Water in May is bread all the year.
- Spain and Italy.

A May flood
Never did good.

A cold May is kindly,
And fills the barn finely.

A wet May
Makes a big load of hay.
- West Shropshire.

May showers bring milk and meal. - Scotland.

A windy May makes a fair year. - Portugal.

Change not a clout
Till May be out.

In the middle of May
comes the tail of the winter. - France.

Shear your sheep in May,
And shear them all away.

Dew	Cool and evening dew in May brings wine and much hay.
Dry	For an east wind in May 'tis your duty to pray.
Snowy	A snowstorm in May Is worth a waggon-load of hay.
Thunder	Many thunderstorms in May, And the farmer sings "Hey! Hey!"
	The more thunder in May, the less in August and September.
Mowing	He who mows in May Will have neither fruit nor hay. - Portugal.
Sowing	He who sows oats in May Gets little that way.

May and June

Look at your corn in May,
And you will come weeping away;
Look at the same in June,
And you'll come home in another tune.
[A proverb alluding to the magical way in which unpromising crops sometimes recover.]

A dry May and a leaking June
Make the farmer whistle a merry tune.

May, June and July

They who bathe in May
Will soon be laid in clay;
They who bathe in June
Will sing a merry tune;
They who bathe in July
Will dance like a fly.

A swarm of bees in May
Is worth a load of hay;
A swarm of bees in June
Is worth a silver spoon;
But a swarm in July
Is not worth a fly.

	A leaking May and a warm June Bring on the harvest very soon. - Scotland. A dry May and a dripping June Bring all things into tune. - Bedfordshire.
May and July	Wet May, dry July. - Germany.
May and August	Mud in May, grain in August. - Spain.
May and September	If May be cold and wet, September will be warm and dry, and vice-versa. - C. L. Prince.
May 1st	Hoar frost on May 1st indicates a good harvest.
	The later the blackthorn in bloom after May 1st, the better the rye and harvest.
(SS. Philip and James)	If it rains on Philip's and Jacob's Day, a fertile year may be expected.
8th	If on the 8th of May it rain, It foretells a wet harvest, men sain. - T. Fuller.
11th, 12th, and 13th	St. Mamertius, St. Pancras, and St. Gervais do not pass without a frost. - France.

Who shears his sheep before St. Gervatius' Day loves more his wool than his sheep.

13th

About this day it is always cold. This is attributed by Professor Erman, of Berlin, to the swarm of meteors through which the earth passes about this time, as at 10th of August, 13th of November, from 5th to 11th of February, and from 10th to 13th of May, lowering the temperature at these times.

17th to 19th (St. Dunstan)	St. Dunstan was a great brewer, and sold himself to the devil, on condition that his Satanic Majesty should blight the apple-trees, and so stop the production of the rival drink - cider. It was, however, stipulated that the blight should be accomplished in three days, the 17th, 18th, and 19th of May, the latter being St. Dunstan's Day. Hence the cold blast which usually comes about this time. - Gardener's Magazine, June 6th, 1891.
19th to 21st	Easterly winds on May 19 to 21 (Old Style) indicate a dry summer. - Professor Boerne's Latin MS. 1677 to 1799.
25th (St. Urban)	At St. Urban gather your walnuts. - Spanish.

JUNE

Calm weather in June
Sets corn in tune.

Calm

It never clouds up in a June night for a rain.
- United States.

Fair

If June be sunny, harvest comes early.

Wheat or barley'll shoot in June
If they bain't no higher ´n a spoon.
- West Somerset.

In the hay season,
when there is no dew,
it indicates rain.

Wet

A cold and wet June
spoils the rest of the year.

June damp and warm
Does the farmer no harm.

A dripping June
Brings all things in tune.

North wind

If north wind blows in June,
good rye harvest.

Harvest

In Scotland an early harvest is expected
when the bramble blossoms early in June.

June and February

When it is hottest in June, it will be coldest in
the corresponding days of the next February.

June and September

A wet June makes a dry September.
- Cornwall.

June 8th

If on the 8th of June it rain,
It foretells a wet harvest, men sain.

8th and 19th (St. Medard, St. Protais)

If it rain on June 8th (St. Medard),
it will rain forty days later;
but if it rain on June 19th (St. Protais),
it rains for forty days after.
- France.

11th (St. Barnabas)

On St. Barnabas
Put a scythe to the grass.

Rain on St. Barnabas' Day good for grapes.

On St. Barnabas' Day
The sun is come to stay.
- Spain.

If St. Vitus's Day be rainy weather,
It will rain for thirty days together.

15th

If it rains on Midsummer Eve,
the filberts will be spoiled.

Before St. John's Day no early crops are worth praising.
- Germany.

24th
(St. John)

Before St. John's Day we pray for rain;
after that we get it anyhow.

If Midsummer Day be never so little rainy, the hazel and walnut will be scarce; corn smitten in many places; but apples, pears, and plums will not be hurt.
- Shepherd's Kalendar.

Rain on St. John's Day, damage to nuts.

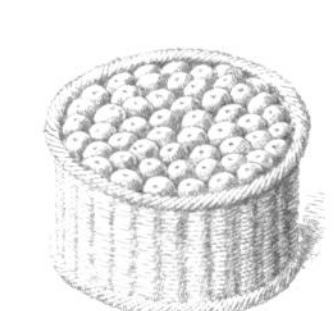

Cut your thistles before St. John,
You will have two instead of one.

Never rued the man
That laid in his fuel before St. John. - T. Fuller.

If it rains on June 27th, it will rain seven weeks.

27th

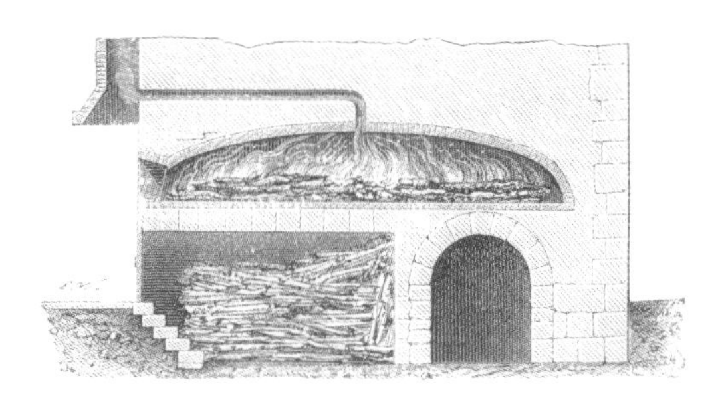

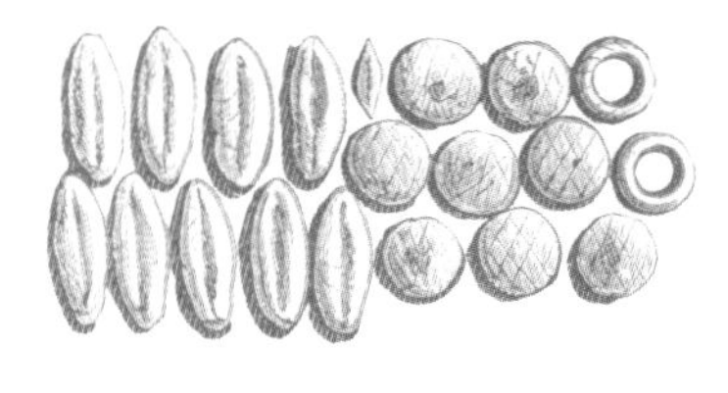

29th (*SS.* Peter and Paul)

If it rains on St. Peter's Day, the bakers will have to carry double flour and single water; if dry, they will carry single flour and double water.

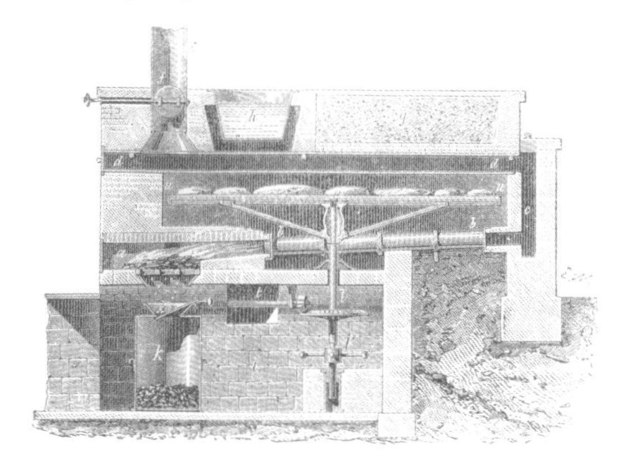

JULY

July, God send thee calm and fayre,
That happy harvest we may see,
With quyet tyme and healthsome ayre,
And man to God may thankful bee.

July, to whom, the dog-star in her train,
St. James gives oysters and St. Swithin rain.
- Churchill.

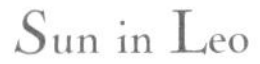

When the sun enters Leo, the greatest heat will then arise.

Sky

Ne'er trust a July sky. - Shetland.

Rye

In July shear your rye.

Thunder

Much thunder in July injures wheat and barley.

July and January

As July, so the next January.

July and August	Whatever July and August do not boil, September cannot fry.
July, August and September	When the months of July, August, and September are unusually hot, January will be the coldest month.
July 1st	If the 1st of July it be rainy weather, It will rain more or less for four weeks together.
1st Friday	The first Friday in July is always wet. - Quoted by C. W. Empson (Folklore Journal).
July 2nd	If it rains on St. Mary's Day, it will rain for four weeks.
July 3rd to Aug. 11th (Dogdays)	As the dog-days commence, so they end. If it rains on first dog-day, it will rain for forty days after. Dog-days bright and clear Indicate a happy year; But when accompanied by rain, For better times our hopes are vain.
4th (St. Martin Bullion)	If Bullion's Day be dry, there will be a good harvest. - Scotland. [St. Martin Bullion, to distinguish it from St. Martin's Day. - P. Dudgeon.] Bullion's Day, gif ye be fair, For forty days 'twill rain nae mair. - Scotland.
10th	If it rains on July 10th, it will rain for seven weeks.

If it rain on the Feast of St. Processus and St. Martin, it suffocates the corn.
- Latin Proverb, "Norwich Doomsday Book."

14th (O.S. July 2nd, SS. Processus and Martinian)

Let not such vulgar tales debase thy mind,
Nor Paul nor Swithin rule the clouds and wind.
- Gay.

15th (St. Swithin)

In this month is St. Swithin's Day,
On which if that it rain they say,
Full forty days after it will
Or more or less some rain distil.
Poor Robin's Almanack, 1697.

St. Swithin is christening the apples.
[This saying is applied to rain on St. Swithin's Day.]

St. Swithin's Day, if ye do rain,
For forty days it will remain;
St. Swithin's Day, an ye be fair,
For forty days 'twill rain nae mair. - Scotland.

All the tears that St. Swithin can cry
St. Bartlemy's dusty mantel wipes dry.

July 15th and August 24th

At St. Vincent the rain ceases and the wind comes.
- France.

19th

Clear on St. Jacob's Day, plenty of fruit.

20th

Rain on St. Margaret's Day will destroy all kinds of nuts. - Germany

(St. Margaret)

22nd (St Mary Magdalene)	The roses are said to begin to fade on this day. Alluding to the wet usually prevalent about the middle of July, the saying is: "St. Mary Magdalene is washing her handkerchief to go to her cousin St. James's fair. - Folk-Lore Journal.
25th (St. James)	Till St. James's Day be come and gone, You may have hops and you may have none.

AUGUST

Dry August and warm
Doth harvest no harm.

Dry

When it rains in August,
it rains honey and wine. - France and Spain.

Wet

A wet August never brings dearth. - Italy.

So many August fogs, so many winter mists.

Fogs

Observe on what day in August the first heavy fog occurs, and expect a hard frost on the same day in October. - United States.

A fog in August indicates a severe winter and plenty of snow.

When the dew is heavy in August, the weather generally remains fair. Thunderstorms in the beginning of August will generally be followed by others all the month.

Dew

As August, so the next February.

August and February

August ripens, September gathers in;
August bears the burden, September the fruit.
- Portugal.

August and September

After Lammas corn ripens as much by night as by day.
[Alluding to the heavy night dews.]

Lammas Day

First week	If the first week in August is unusually warm, the winter will be white and long.
10th (St. Lawrence)	If on St. Lawrence's Day the weather be fine, fair autumn and good wine may be hoped for. - Germany.
15th (Assumption)	On St. Mary's Day sunshine Brings much and good wine.

24th (St. Bartholomew)	If this day be misty, the morning beginning with a hoar-frost, the cold weather will soon come, and a hard winter. - Shepherd's Kalendar. If it rains this day, it will rain the forty days after. - Rome. St. Bartlemy's mantle wipes dry All the tears that St. Swithin can cry. If Bartlemy's Day be fair and clear, They hope for a prosperous autumn that year. Thunderstorms after Bartholomew's Day are more violent.

SEPTEMBER

September dries up ditches or breaks down bridges. - Portugal.	Dry or wet
'Tis September's sun which causes the black list upon the antelope's back. - Bombay.	Sun
As September, so the coming March.	September and March
When September has been rainy, the following May is generally dry; and when May is dry, the following September is apt to be wet. - Professor Boerne's Latin MS. 1677 to 1799.	September and May
A wet September, drought for next summer, famine, and no crops. - California.	Wet
Heavy September rains bring drought. - United States.	Rain

Rain in September is good for the farmer, but poison to the vine-growers. - German.

September rain is much liked by the farmer.

September rain good for crops and vines.

Storms	If the storms in September clear off warm, all the storms of the following winter will be warm.
Cold	When a cold spell occurs in September and passes without a frost, a frost will not occur until the same time in October.
Thunder	Thunder in September indicates a good crop of grain and fruit for next year.
Fodder	Preserve your fodder in September and your cow will fatten. - Portugal

September blow soft till the fruit's in the loft.
November take flail, let ships no more sail.

September and November

Fair on September 1st, fair for the month.

Sept. 1st

St. Giles finishes the walnuts. - Spain.

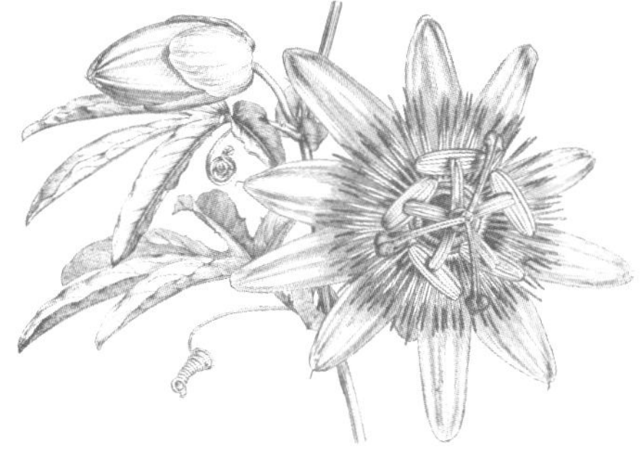

The passion flower blossomed about this time. The flower is said to present a resemblance to the cross or rood, the nails, and the crown of thorns, used at the Crucifixion. - Circle of the Seasons

14th (Holyrood)

If dry be the buck's horn
On Holyrood morn,
'Tis worth a kist of gold;
But if wet it be seen
Ere Holyrood e'en.
Bad harvest is foretold. - Yorkshire.

If the hart and the hind meet dry and part dry
on Rood Day fair,
For sax weeks, of rain there'll be nae mair.
- Scotland.

On Holy-Cross Day
Vineyards are gay.
- Spain.

Three windy days

There are generally three consecutive windy days about the middle of September, which have been called by the Midland millers the windy days of barley harvest.

15th

This day is said to be fine in six years out of seven.
- T. Forster (Perennial Calendar).

19th

If on September 19th there is a storm from the south, a mild winter may be expected.
- Derby.

A quiet week before the autumn equinox and after, the temperature will continue higher than usual into the winter.

21st

These three days of September rule the weather for October, November, and December.

20th, 21st, and 22nd

St. Matthee,
Shut up the bee.

21st (St. Matthew)

St. Matthew's rain fattens pigs and goats. - Spain.

St. Matthew
Brings on the cold dew.

St. Matthew makes the days and nights equal.
- Spain.

Matthew's Day bright and clear
Brings good wine in next year.

South wind on September 21st indicates that the rest of the autumn will be warm.

St. Matthew
and
St. Matthias

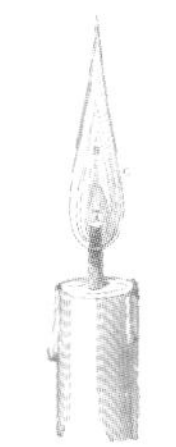

St. Matthew,
get candlesticks new;
St. Mathi,
lay candlesticks by.

29th
(Michaelmas
Day)

So many days old the moon is on Michaelmas Day, so many floods after.
- Howell.

If St. Michael brings many acorns,
Christmas will cover the fields with snow.

St. Michael's rain does not stay long in the sky.
- France.

On Michaelmas Day
the devil puts his foot on the blackberries.
- North of Ireland.

If it does not rain on
St. Michael's and Gallus,
a dry spring is indicated
for the next year.

OCTOBER

Dry your barley in October,
Or you'll always be sober.
[Because if this is not done there will be no malt.
- Swainson.]

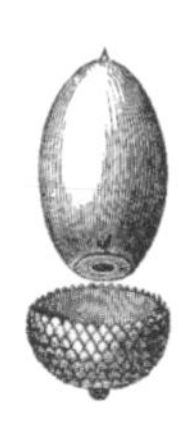

Wind	A good October and a good blast, To blow the hog acorn and mast.
Fine	There are always nineteen (some say twenty-one) fine days in October. - Kent.
Rain	Much rain in October, much wind in December.
Frosts, etc.	If October bring heavy frosts and winds, then will January and February be mild.
Snow	If the first snow falls on moist, soft earth, it indicates a small harvest; but if upon hard, frozen soil, a good harvest.
Fogs	For every fog in October a snow in the winter, heavy or light according as the fog is heavy or light.

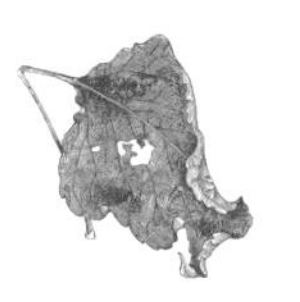

If in the fall of the leaves in October many of them wither on the boughs and hang there, it betokens a frosty winter and much snow.

Leaves

Warm October, cold February.

October and February

As the weather in October,
so will it be in the next March.

October and March

Plenty of rain in October and November on the North Pacific coast indicates a mild winter; little rain in these months will be followed by a severe winter.

October and winter

Moon

Full moon in October without frost, no frost till full moon in November.

When birds and badgers are fat in October, expect a cold winter. - United States.

October 18th (St. Luke)

St. Luke's little summer.

There is often about this time a spell of fine, dry weather, and this has received the name of St. Luke's little summer.

28th (SS. Simon and Jude)

This day was anciently accounted as certain to be rainy.

On St. Jude's Day
The oxen may play.

NOVEMBER

Flowers in bloom late in autumn
indicate a bad winter.

Flowers

November take flail,
Let ships no more sail. - Tusser.

Windy

When in November the water rises,
it will show itself the whole winter.

Water

If there's ice in November that will bear a duck,
There'll be nothing after but sludge and muck.

Cold

A heavy November snow will last till April.
- New England.

Thunder in November, a fertile year to come.

Thunder

Thunder in November on the Northern lakes is
taken as an indication that the lakes will remain open
till at least the middle of December.
- United States.

November and March

As November, so the following March.

Nov. 1st (All Saints' Day)

In Sweden there is often about this time some warm weather, called "The All Saints' Rest."

On the 1st of November, if the weather hold clear,
An end of wheat sowing do make for the year.

If All Saints' Day will bring out the winter,
St. Martin's Day will bring out Indian summer.
- United States.

If on All Saints' Day the beech nut be found dry, we shall have a hard winter; but if the nut be wet and not light, we may expect a wet winter.

11th (St. Martin)

If this day be fair, the next winter will bring but little rain and snow along with it; but if the first half of the day be clear and the other cloudy, the beginning of winter will accordingly be fair, but its end and spring will turn out rigorous and disagreeable.
- Kalm ("Travels in North America").

If ducks do slide at Hollantide,
At Christmas they will swim;
If ducks do swim at Hollantide,
At Christmas they will slide.

If it is at Martinmas fair dry and cold, the cold in winter will not last long.

If the geese at Martin's Day stand on ice, they will walk in mud at Christmas.

If the leaves of the trees and grape vines do not fall before Martin's Day, a cold winter may be expected.

Wind north-west at Martinmas, severe winter to come.
- Huntingdonshire.

If the wind is in the south-west at Martinmas, it keeps there till after Candlemas, with a mild winter up to then and no snow to speak of.
- Midland Counties.

At St. Martin's Day
Winter is on his way. - France.

Expect St. Martin's summer, halcyon days
[i.e. fine weather at Martinmas.]
- Shakespeare (1 Henry VI. i. 2).

November 11th
December 25th

'Tween Martinmas and Yule
Water's wine in every pool. - Scotland.

Nov. 21st

As November 21st, so is the winter.

25th

As at Catherine foul or fair, so will be the next February.

DECEMBER

December cold with snow, good for rye.

Cold

Thunder in December presages fine weather.

Thunder

December's frost and January's flood
Never boded the husbandman's good.

December and January

Look at the weathercock on St. Thomas's Day at twelve o'clock, and see which way the wind is, for there it will stick for the next (lunar) quarter.

21st (St. Thomas)

Lucy light, Lucy light,
Shortest day and longest night.

(St. Lucia)

Frost on the shortest day is said to indicate a severe winter.
- Lancashire.

Frost

25th

A green Christmas makes a fat churchyard.

A green Christmas brings a heavy harvest.
- Rutland.

At Christmas meadows green, at Easter covered with frost.

A clear and bright sun on Christmas Day foretelleth a peaceable year and plenty; but if the wind grow stormy before sunset, it betokeneth sickness in the spring and autumn quarters.

Christmas sunshine

If the sun shine through the apple-tree on Christmas Day, there will be an abundant crop in the following year.

The shepherd would rather see his wife enter the stable on Christmas Day than the sun.
- Germany

Light Christmas,* light wheatsheaf;
Dark Christmas, heavy wheatsheaf.

Moon

If windy on Christmas Day,
trees will bring much fruit.

Windy

A warm Christmas, a cold Easter;
A green Christmas, a white Easter. - Germany.

Christmas and Easter

So far as the sun shines on Christmas Day,
So far will the snow blow in May. - Germany

Christmas and May

Christmas wet, empty granary and barrel.

Wet

If it snows during Christmas night,
the crops will do well.

Snow

If at Christmas ice hangs on the willow,
clover may be cut at Easter.

Ice

If ice will bear a man before Christmas, it will not bear a mouse afterwards. [Also said of a goose and duck.]

* If full moon about Christmas Day.

Blackbird	When the blackbird sings before Christmas, she will cry before Candlemas. - Meath.
Christmas and Candlemas	A windy Christmas and a calm Candlemas are signs of a good year.
Wine	If on Christmas night the wine ferments heavily in the barrels, a good wine year is to follow.

Thunder during Christmas week indicates that there will be much snow during the winter.

Thunder

These twelve days are said to be the keys of the weather for the whole year.

Dec. 25th to Jan.5th

There was a superstitious practice in France on Christmas Day of placing twelve onions, representing the twelve months. Each onion had a pinch of salt on the top; and if the salt had melted by Epiphany, the month corresponding was put down as sure to be wet; while if the salt remained, the month was to be dry.

Christmas to Epiphany

If it rain much during the twelve days after Christmas, it will be a wet year.

Dec. 26th	St. Stephen's Day windy, bad for next year's grapes.
28th (Innocents' Day)	The "Shepherd's Kalendar" mentions that if it be lowering and wet on Childermas Day there will be scarcity; while if the day be fair it promises plenty.
31st	If New Years Eve night wind blow south, It betokeneth warmth and growth; If west, much milk and fish in the sea; If north, much cold and storms there will be; If east, the trees will bear much fruit; If north-east, flee it man and brute.

EQUINOX

As the wind and weather, at the equinoxes, so will they be for the next three months.

As the equinoctial storms clear, so will all storms clear for the six months.

Wind north-east or north at noon of the vernal equinox, no fine weather before midsummer. If westerly or south westerly, fine weather till midsummer.

Vernal equinox, wind N.E. and S.W.

If the wind is north-east at vernal equinox, it will be a good season for wheat and a poor one for other kinds of corn; but if south or south-west, it will be good for other corn, but bad for wheat.

Equinoctial gales

The vernal equinoctial gales are stronger than the autumnal.

If near the time of the equinox it blows in the day, it generally hushes towards evening.

Proverbs Relating to Various Moveable Feasts

Shrove Tuesday	So much as the sun shineth on Pancake Tuesday, the like will shine every day in Lent.
	Thunder on Shrove Tuesday foretelleth wind, store of fruit, and plenty.
	When the sun is shining on Shrovetide Day, it is meant well for rye and peas.
Ash Wednesday	Wherever the wind lies on Ash Wednesday, it continues during all Lent.
Lent	Dry Lent, fertile year.
Late	Never come Lent, never come winter. - Herefordshire.
Palm Sunday	If the weather is not clear on Palm Sunday, it means a bad year.
Good Friday	Rain on Good Friday foreshows a fruitful year.
Good Friday and Easter Day	A wet Good Friday and a wet Easter Day Make plenty of grass, but very little hay.

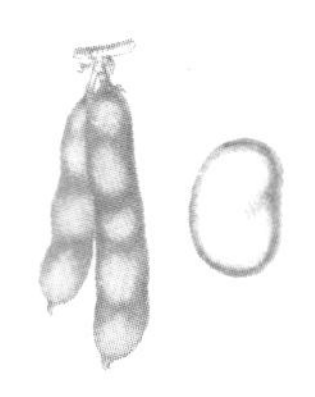

Late Easter, long, cold spring.
- Sussex.

Easter

Rain at Easter gives slim fodder. - United States.

A rainy Easter betokens a good harvest.
- France.

If the sun shines on Easter Day, it shines on Whitsunday likewise.

Easter Day

It was once a popular belief, and a very pretty one, that the sun danced upon Easter Day.

Past Easter frost,
Fruit not lost.

Frost

A good deal of rain upon Easter Day
Gives a good crop of grass, but little good hay.
- Hertfordshire.

Rain

Such weather as there is on Easter Day there will be at harvest.

Weather

[As a correspondent in "Notes and Queries" (July 10, 1875) points out, this superstition may have arisen from the pagan sacrifice to the goddess Eostre (from which name the Venerable Bede says "Easter" is derived), a sacrifice made about the vernal equinox, with a view to a good harvest.]

Easter come early, or Easter come late,
Is sure to make the old cow quake. - Herefordshire.

First Sunday after

The first Sunday after Easter settles the weather for the whole summer. - Sweden.

Pastor Sunday (second after Easter)

If it rains on Pastor Sunday, it will rain every Sunday until Pentecost (Whitsunday).

Holy Thursday

Fine on Holy Thursday, wet on Whit-Monday; fine on Whit-Monday, wet on Holy Thursday.
- Huntingdonshire.

As the weather on Ascension Day,
so may be the entire autumn.

Ascension Day

If fair weather from Easter to Whitsuntide,
the butter will be cheap.

Easter to Whitsuntide

Corpus Christi Day clear
Gives a good year.

Corpus Christi (Thursday after Trinity Sunday)

Whitsuntide rain, blessing for wine.

Rain at Whitsuntide is said to make the meat mildewed.

Whitsunday (called also Pentecost - the fiftieth day after Easter)

Strawberries at Whitsuntide
indicate good wine.

Whitsunday bright and clear
Will bring a fertile year.

Whitsunday wet, Christmas fat.

Whitsunday and Christmas

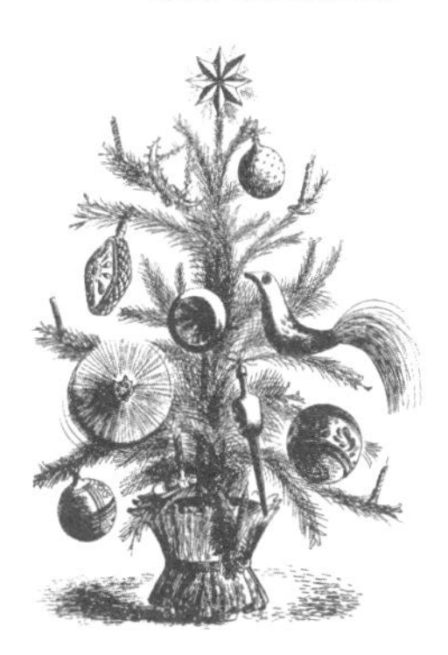

Proverbs Relating to the Months Generally

Month — The month that comes in good
will go out bad.

Character of — January fierce, cold, and frosty,
February moist and aguish,
March dusty,
April rainy,
May pretty, gay, and windy,
Bring an abundant harvest.
- France.

Lunar Months — The endings and beginnings of the lunar months are more terrible at night and are more stormy than other parts of the month.
- Theophrastus
("Signs, etc." J. G. Wood's Translation).

Months with R — In Scotland the rule
for using household fires is:
All the months with an R in them.

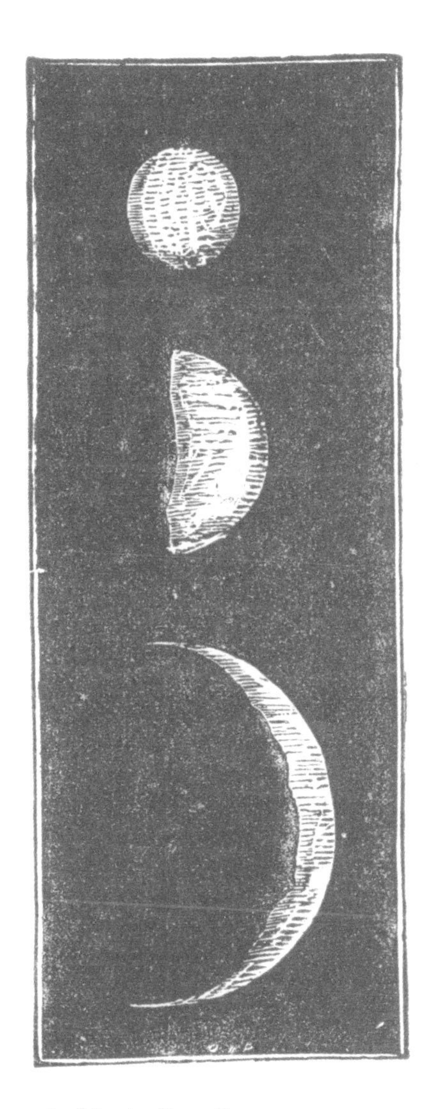

Days of the Week

Author's Note: These sayings, though for the most part purely superstitious, I have inserted in order to complete the collection.

Wednesday clear

When the sun sets clear on Wednesday,
expect clear weather the rest of the week.

Thursday

On Thursday at three
Look out, and you'll see
What Friday will be.
- South Devon.

Friday

Friday's a day as'll have his trick,
The fairest or foulest day o' the wik [week].
- Shropshire.

Friday and Sunday

If on Friday it rain,
'Twill on Sunday again;
If Friday be clear,
Have for Sunday no fear.

If the sun sets clear on Friday,
it will blow before Sunday night.

If the sun sets clear on Friday,
generally expect rain before Monday.

There is never a Saturday without some sunshine.	Saturday
If it rains on Sunday before Mass, it will rain all the week.	Sunday
Sunday clearing, clear till Wednesday.	Clearing
If sunset on Sunday is cloudy, it will rain before Wednesday.	Sunset
When it storms on the first Sunday in the month, it will storm every Sunday.	First in month

Last in month

The last Sunday in the month indicates the weather of the next month.

Day misty

A misty morning may have a fine day.
- T. Fuller.

Cold

When there are three days cold, expect three days colder.

Fine

A warm and serene day, which we say is too fine for the season, betokens a speedy reverse.
- F. K. Robinson (Whitby Glossary).

Days and nights

Frosty nights and hot sunny days
Set the cornfields all in a blaze.

Day and night

A blustering night, a fair day.
- C. Harvey.

A bad day has a good night.

A day should be praised at night.
- Norway.

Evening

Praise a fair day at even.

Night and Morning

What have we got here? A cloudy night and a red morning! That betokens rough weather.
Sir W. Scott ("Pirate", ch. xii.).

Warm

If a warm noon succeeds a cold morning (on the Delaware) it is a sign of a change in the weather.
- Kalm ("Travels in North America").

If a change of weather occur when the sun or moon is crossing the meridian, it is for twelve hours at least. - Nautical.

Noon change

Twilight looming indicates rain.

Twilight

If the weather change at night,
it will not last when the day breaks.
- France.

Night

A day in England is generally
much like the one before.
[This proves a safer scheme of weather prophecy than any other system, for the weather does not totally change nearly so often as people imagine.]

Day

Between twelve and two
You'll see what the day will do. - Cornwall.

12 and 2

Rain at seven, fine at eleven;
Rain at eight, not fine till eight.

7 and 11

List of Common Plants

The two following lists of the average dates for first flowering of plants in central England generally have been kindly furnished by Ed Mawley, Esq. Past President Royal Meteorological Society. The forwardness of any season may be judged by the punctuality of the appearance of the blossoms.

WILD PLANTS

Hazel	February 13
Coltsfoot	March 9
Wood Anemone	March 29
Blackthorn	April 12
Garlic Hedge Mustard	April 23
Horse Chestnut	May 7
Hawthorn	May 10
White Ox Eye	May 25
Dog Rose	June 6
Black Knapweed	June 23
Harebell	July 7
Greater Bindweed	July 7
Ivy	September 27

- "Quarterly Journal Royal Meteorological Society", April, 1897.

Garden Plants

Average dates of first flowering, etc. of plants in Mr. Mawley's garden at Berkhamsted, Herts.

Winter Aconite	January 24
Double Snowdrop	February 10
Yellow Crocus	February 24
Chinodoxa Lucilis (Glory of the Snow)	March 10
Wild Cherry	April 21
Blenheim Orange Apple	May 5
Common Lilac	May 9
Wild Dog Rose	June 4
First Tea Rose	June 12
First Hybrid Perpetual Rose	June 17
Dahlias killed by frost	November 2

FLOWERS
(which should be open on certain saints' days.)

February 2(Candlemas),	Snowdrop
February 14 (St. Valentine),	Crocus
March 25 (Lady Day)	Daffodil
April 23 (St. George)	Harebell
May 3 (Holy Cross)	Crowfoot
June 11 (St. Barnabas)	Ragged Robin
June 24 (St. John the Bap t)	Scarlet
July 15 (St. Swithin)	Lily [Lychnis]
July 20 (St. Margaret)	Poppy
July 22 (St. Magdalene),	Rose
August 1 (Lammas)	Camomile
August 15 (Assumption)	Virgin's Bower
August 24 (St. Bartholomew)	Sunflower
September 14 (Holyrood)	Passion Flower
September 29 (Michaelmas)	Michaelmas Daisy
November 25 (St. Catherine)	Laurel
December 25 (Christmas)	Ivy and Holly

And the times at which, in ordinary fine weather,
they open and close their petals. Their opening later or closing earlier than the usual time is a sign of rain, and vice versa.

	OPENS.	CLOSES.
	A.M.	P.M.
Goatsbeard	3 to 5	9 to 10
Succory	4 to 5	8 to 9
Ox Tongue	4 to 5	12
Naked Poppy	5	7
Day Lily	5	7 to 8

Sow Thistle	5	11 to 12
Blue Thistle	5	12
Dandelion	5 to 6	8 to 9
Convolvulus	5 to 6	4 to 5
Spotted Hawkweed	6 to 7	4 to 5
Lettuce	7	10
White Water Lily	7	5
African Marigold	7	3 to 4
Pimpernel	7 to 8	2 to 3
Proliferous Pink	8	6
Mouse Ear	8	2
Field Marigold	9	3
Chickweed	9 to 10	9 to 10
Caroline Mallow	9 to 10	12 to1

Birds

And the times at which they usually appear in the South of England.

Wryneck	Middle of March
Smallest Willow Wren	Latter end of March
House Swallow	Middle of April
Martin	Middle of April
Sand Martin	Middle of April
Blackcap	Middle of April
Nightingale	Beginning of April
Cuckoo	Middle of April
Middle Willow Wren	Middle of April
Whitethroat	Middle of April
Redstart	Middle of April
Great Plover, or Stone Curlew	End of March
Grasshopper Lark	Middle of April
Swift	Latter end of April
Largest Willow Wren	End of April
Fern Owl	Latter end of May
Flycatcher	Middle of May

- T. Forster ("Perennial Calendar").

Winter birds.

TIMES OF THEIR ARRIVAL.

Ring Ouzel — Soon after Michaelmas

Redwing — Middle of October

Fieldfare — October and November

Royston Crow — October

Woodcock — Keeps arriving all Oct/Nov

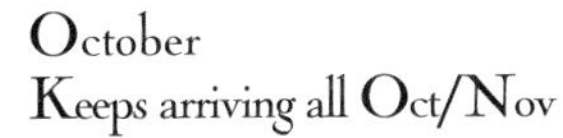

Snipe	The same (some breed here).
Jack Snipe	The same (some breed here).

Pigeon, or Stock Dove	End of November (some abide here all the year).
Wood Pigeon, or Ring Dove	Some abide all the year; some arrive in spring; others perform partial migrations.

- T. Forster ("Perennial Calendar").

Indications of spring near Stratton, Norfolk.
By Robert Marsham, F.R.S.
Continued by members of his family for more than a hundred years.

	AVERAGE DATES.
Swallows arrive	April 14.
Cuckoo first heard	April 23.
Nightingale first heard	April 27.

Song or migration of birds and first appearance of insects.
Average dates for British Isles, 1891-96.

Song Thrush first heard	February 2
Swallow first seen	April 17
Cuckoo first heard	April 20
Nightingale first heard	April 21
Flycatcher first seen	May 13
Swallow last seen	October 13
Honey Bee appears	February 28
Wasp appears	April 7.
Small White Butterfly	April 11.
Orange-tip Butterfly	May 4.
Meadow-brown Butterfly	June 7.

- E. Mawley
("Quarterly Journal Royal Meteorological Society", April, 1897).

Weather Lore

A Collection of

Proverbs, Sayings & Rules

Concerning the Weather

Also in this series:

Volume II

Sun, Moon & Stars

The Elements - Sky, Air, Sound, Heat

Volume III

The Elements

Clouds, Mists, Haze, Dew, Fog, Rain, Rainbows

Volume IV

The Elements

Wind, Sea, Thunder & Lightning, Frost, Hail, Snow, Ice

Volume V

Flora & Fauna

Volume VI

Instruments of Measure